Guide to Zoom

A quick guide to learn how to install and use Zoom in 10 minutes

(unofficial guide)

Manuel Martín

Title: Guide to Zoom

2020 © Manuel Martín.

Text © Manuel Martín.

Cover illustration © Manuel Martín.

Review © Manuel Martín.

1st edition

for any poor results you may obtain by implementing the techniques or following the guidelines set forth for you in this book.

All products, websites and company names mentioned in this report are trademarks or copyrights of their respective owners. The author is not associated or affiliated with them in any way. The product, website and company names mentioned are also not sponsored, endorsed or approved by this product.

Content

If you find helpful this guide,
A <u>little review</u> would help me a lot.

Thank you very much

What is Zoom Meetings and what is it used for?

Zoom Video is a video conferencing or virtual meeting system, accessible from computers and smartphones.

It is employed to make video calls, online conferences, and any type of activities that cannot be done physically. It is an extremely valuable tool in these times, even more so with the rise of technology.

Whether you are an entrepreneur, self-employed, or employee, it is highly recommended that you familiarize yourself with this type of application. For both work and family environments

What do you need?

1. **Install** Zoom. You can choose from:
     - A desktop Computer
     - A laptop
     - A Tablet
     - A smartphone
2. It is equally convenient to have a **headset** to avoid being disturbed.
3. **Webcam** to be seen. Ordinarily, laptops and smartphones have it built-in.
4. **A microphone** to be heard. The laptops equally have them incorporated.

Tips for proper use

To take care of our physical health while using Zoom.

Here are some tips:

https://www.wikihow.com/Sit-at-a-Computer

And here they are the recommendations of University of Granada (Spanish)

https://ssprl.ugr.es/pages/servicio_prevencion_riesgos_laborales/tripticoposturaordenador

Create an account and install Zoom on Desktop or Laptop

Go to https://zoom.us/signup and register by entering the data requested.

Now, select one of the two options:

- Manual registration; by entering your email and confirming the registration.
- Registration via the link from our Google or Facebook account (**recommended**)

Registration through Gmail account (Google). Step 1

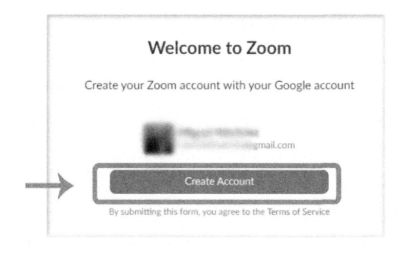

Registration through Gmail account (Google). Step 2

- The next step is to install the Zoom client on your computer. To perform this, go to https://zoom.us/download, and download "Zoom Client for Meetings"

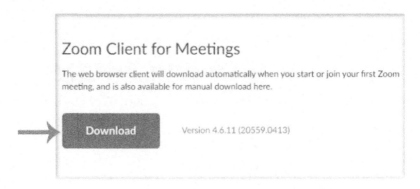

Client download. Step 1

If we are downloading with the Google Chrome browser, we will see it in the lower-left corner. We wait until downloading is complete then we click on that.

Client download. Step 2

Once the program is open, we go to the Login section, and log in again with our Google account, as we have done formerly.

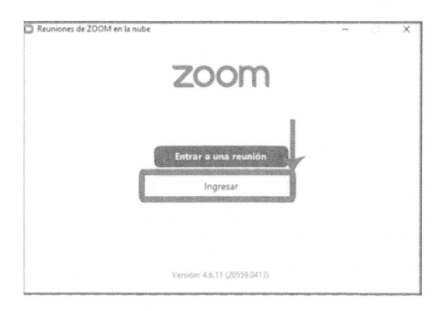

Log in. Step 1 (you should see the English client)

Log in. Step 2 (you should see the English client)

Now, a pop-up window will open. We click "Open Zoom Meetings".

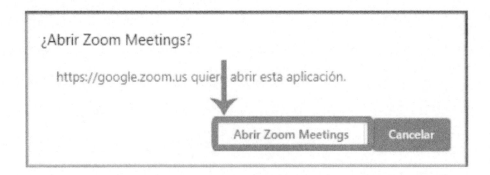

We already have our Zoom Client installed and ready to use.

Create an account and install Zoom on Smartphone and Tablets

The first thing is to download the application.

For **Android**, we click on the following link:

https://play.google.com/store/apps/details?id=us.zoom.videomeetingsl=es_419

If it does not work, do it manually looking for "Zoom" at https://play.google.com/

For **iPhone and other Apple devices**, click here:

https://apps.apple.com/es/app/zoom-cloud-meetings/id546505307

For any other questions, please go to the Zoom download center:

https://zoom.us/support/download

Now, if we already have an account, we click on "Login", and if not, click on **"Register",** and follow the registration steps we already looked at.

Once we have reached the end, we will have to confirm our email by clicking on the link sent to us via email.

After that, we can log in to our account using the "**Login**" option.

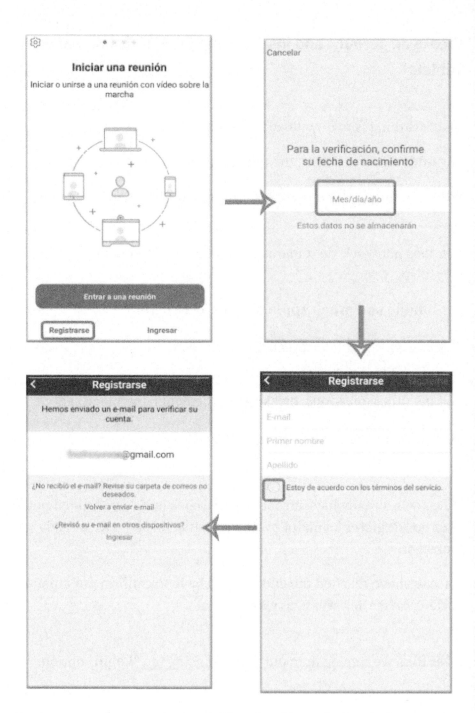

Register account from Android (You should see the English version).

Starting to use Zoom

Let's see how to use Zoom on a computer. Some functions may be unavailable on the smartphone, as a room creator or virtual background. Otherwise, it's very similar, and in any case easier to use.

Adding contacts

Go to the "Contacts" tab and click on the "+" button, and "Add a contact".

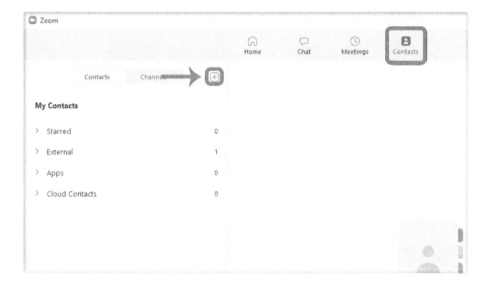

Now we can click on "Copy invitation", so we can paste the link into any site (WhatsApp, email, website etc.) and invite someone to join Zoom. Alternatively, we can send the invitation directly to a friend/family member.

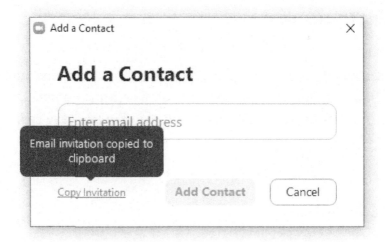

In this section, we can see and manage our contacts.

Any contact we add will appear in "External Contacts". We have to click on their name then on "Chat" to start chatting.

Create channels

As an entrepreneur, teacher, or for any small or significant meeting, you can create specific channels and initiate a meeting at any time. Once the channel is created, you can add contacts.

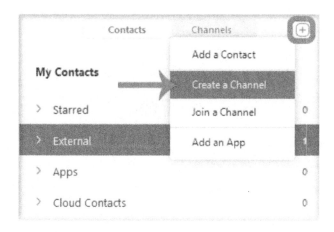

Send messages and files to contacts

To send files to contacts, you need to open a chat conversation with him or her.

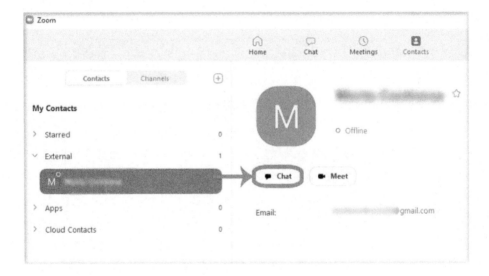

Once inside, it's as simple as clicking on "File" and choosing among the various sources offered by the program.

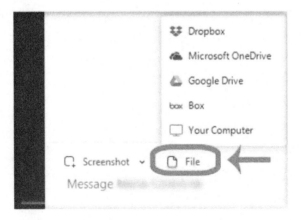

Create or join a meeting

Schedule a meeting

This is a very interesting option. We can program a meeting with details such as starting time, duration, recurrence and initiate a meeting with some frequency, and even assign a password to make it private.

Browse through the numerous options to select the one that best suits the situation.

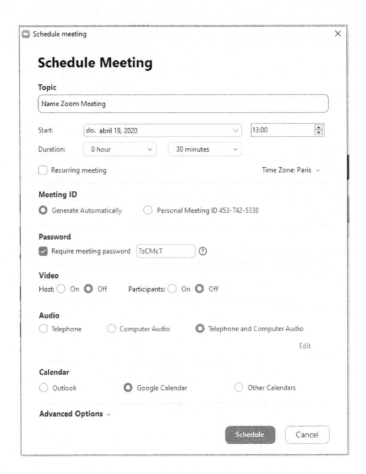

Create a meeting immediately

Let's go to the Zoom home screen and click on "New Meeting".

Here, it is important to select the option "Test Speaker and Microphone" to make sure that our sound is correctly configured and we can hear other people.

We'll have a sound check where we should hear a sound through our speakers. We click on "Yes" if we hear it. If not, we will have to make sure that our speakers are correctly connected and do not have any incidence with the sound of our computer. If we possess several sound output systems, (Desktop speakers, built-in monitor speaker, headphones connected, etc.) make sure you choose the right one.

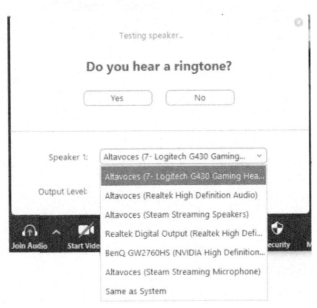

And now, the microphone test. Make sure it is properly connected and configured. If you have any problem in either case, try to search Google or YouTube for a video or tutorial depending on your problem and operating system. There are a lot of tutorials on the web.

Once completed the test, we can select "Join with computer Audio" and once inside, we can check the status of speakers and microphone in the next option:

To invite someone to your meeting, you can do it in several ways. Go to the top left corner of the meeting screen and click on the information symbol. We can now copy the "Meeting ID" through WhatsApp or Telegram or any other application to manually access the meeting, or provide the link to access the meeting directly by clicking on it (**recommended**). This way Zoom will automatically open. To complete this, click on "Copy URL".

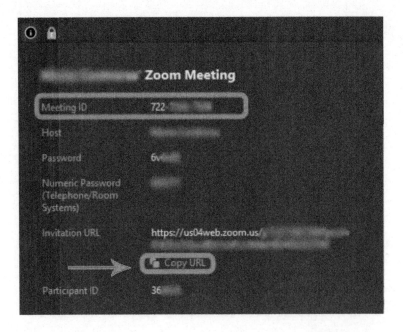

When someone enters the meeting, you'll have to **admit** him/her by clicking on the notification that appears, since by default they appear in the waiting room.

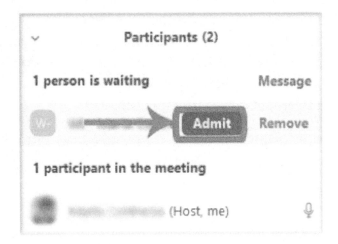

It can be interesting to make a Host, so he will be assigned all the permissions of a room creator host, and thus be able to moderate the room. Click "More" and select "Make Host".

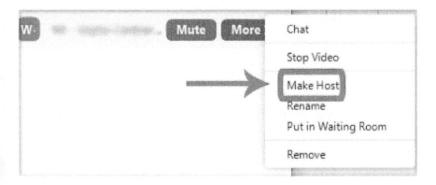

Join a meeting

Once we click on "Join", it will ask us for a meeting ID that the host should have provided us, and whose format is similar to XXX-XXXX-XXX. **Ask the host for the** ID to access the room. The easiest way is to **provide the link via WhatsApp or Telegram to click** and access directly. You will be able to choose the name you use to enter the room.

If for some reason, you do not wish to be heard or seen, you can explore the options below: "Do no connect to Audio" or "Turn off my Video".

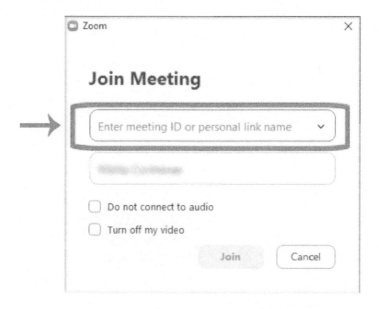

IMPORTANT NOTE FOR ANDROID USERS: If you access a meeting from a smartphone or tablet, you will need to click on "Audio" in the lower-left corner and then "Call via device audio". **Otherwise, you will not be heard and will not be able to hear anybody until you do this step.**

Later, you can mute your microphone if you wish.

Options bar during a meeting

As a meeting manager, the bar looks like this

From left to right, we can see:

- **Mute**: to activate/deactivate your audio.
- **Start video:** activate/deactivate your video.
- **Security**: allow participants options such as screen sharing, chatting, renaming etc.
- **Manage Participants**: members of the current meeting.
- **Chat**: to chat during the meeting. This is effective for people who won't be able to connect the audio or video because they do not have a microphone, webcam, or encounter technical problems in this regard.
- **Screen sharing**: This option allows you to share what you see on your screen with others: presentations, videos, photos, etc.

- o **In the basic menu** you can share any window you have opened, such as photos, presentations, videos etc. This option is the most used in most cases.
- o **In the advanced menu, you will be** able to share only a part of the screen of your choice, in addition to being able to share the audio generated by your computer without the video.

- o In the "Files" menu you can send a file such as a PDF, a PPT presentation, or an MP3 or MP4 file.

To finish sharing, just click on "Stop Sharing".

Whiteboard Option

In Screen Sharing > Basic Menu, we can find the whiteboard option.

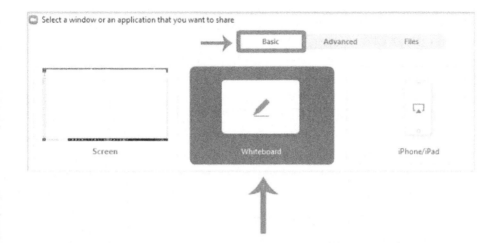

Here, we can share a virtual whiteboard, ideal for any type of class that requires notes and explanations.

The interface is shown as follows:

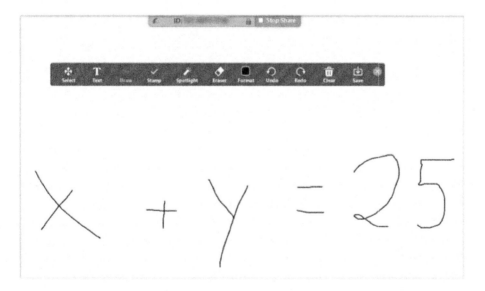

We have an option bar to select, include text, draw, erase, color, etc.

We additionally have the option "Save" to save our photo from the board on our computer.

Continuing with the options on our main bar:

- **_Record_**: Record the current meeting to make it available for later. You can store the file in MP4 at the end of the meeting
  - o When we are done, we will click on "End meeting" and our file will be saved on our computer. By default, the destination folder will be opened. If not, it will be saved to C:\Users\ (your user) \Documents\zoom.
  - o They can also be accessed via Configuration > Recording >Open.

- **_Reactions_**: Introduce emoticons to encourage the interlocutors.

As a participant, the options bar is practically the same. In this case, the "Security" function is unavailable.

Virtual background option

If you have a green room background that contrasts with you, Zoom can do a **virtual background** appears. This is something that looks exceptionally good and avoids having to reveal the background of your room, providing us with the option to choose between diverse landscapes, or even upload a photo or video of our own.

To activate this option, we log into our Zoom profile as we have seen before, by going to https://zoom.us/signin and log in with our Google account.

Once logged in, go to "Settings" and search for "Virtual background". Turn it on.

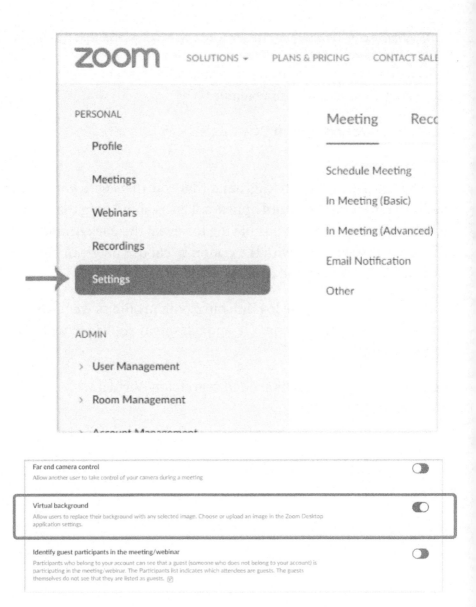

Now, we try finding an evenly colored green sheet. It doesn't have to be exactly green, but the results are optimized for this color. Try doing it with the colors you have available. There must be no objects, so that the background you choose contrasts with our green.

Make sure the light is not too overly bright or too dark.

To access the virtual background, go to the Configuration > Virtual background > Choose the virtual background (**NOTE: By clicking on "+" you can upload your background or video**) > Click on "I have a green screen" and exit.

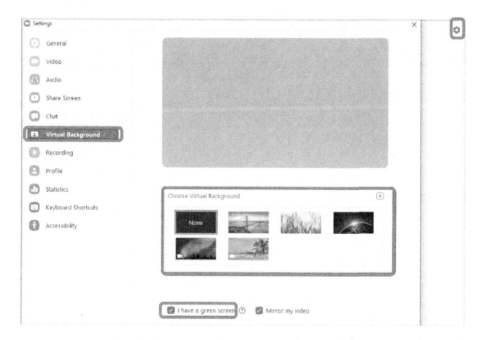

It may seem that we are on the beach or in the mountains, and the result will be like this:

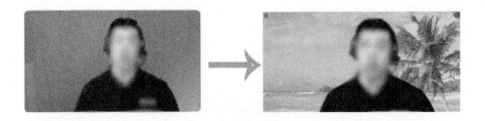

If you want to vary the background during a meeting, go to video > video settings.

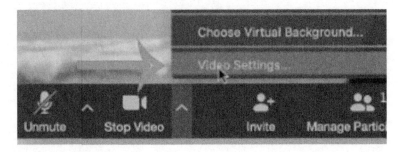

Remote Control

During a meeting, you can request for remote control of someone's computer. This option is immensely useful when you are explaining something to someone else and they are unable to do it successfully: we can take over their mouse and keyboard to execute actions on their computer.

To activate it, the person from whom we want to remotely control the computer must **share their screen** by using the "Share screen" option.

Once this is executed, you should go to the menu at the top of the screen and click on **View options > Request Remote Control.**

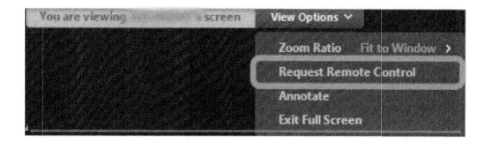

The other person must ACCEPT to start the remote control and we can now control their computer.

To finish, go back to the "View Options" menu and stop the remote control.

Keyboard shortcuts

In Configuration > Keyboard shortcuts menu, we can find the shortcuts to receive a more efficient experience, so by pressing the key combinations we can execute certain functions and save time.

Take a look to see which one best suit your meeting features.

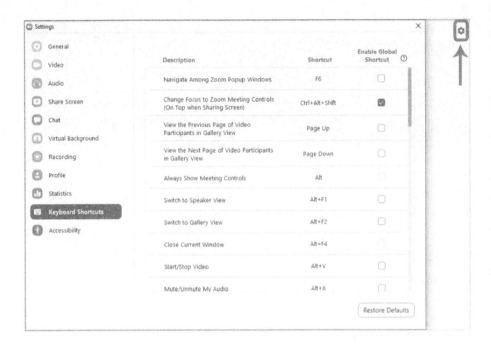

Final

And so far, we have seen an introduction to the most famous videoconferencing program in existence today (basic account)

There are many more features that you can investigate, but 90% of people use them with what we have seen in this book.

If you have found this guide useful and would like to show me your appreciation, you can leave a **brief review** on Amazon.com.

That would help me a LOT

Thank you

Manuel Martín

Printed in Great Britain
by Amazon

39760807R10030